WITHDRAWN FROM
THE LIBRARY

UNIVERSITY OF
WINCHESTER

KA 0204820 5

D1341772

A tribute to The Man from Snowy River

A tribute to The Man from Snowy River

David Parker's magnificent
photography illustrates a "Banjo" Paterson selection

With an introduction by Clement Semmler

ANGUS & ROBERTSON PUBLISHERS

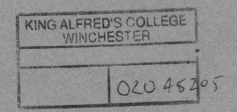

KING ALFRED'S COLLEGE
WINCHESTER

020 45205

Angus & Robertson Publishers
London • Sydney • Melbourne • Singapore • Manila

This book is copyright. Apart from any fair dealing for the
purposes of private study, research, criticism or review, as
permitted under the Copyright Act, no part may be reproduced
by any process without written permission. Inquiries should be
addressed to the publishers.

First published by Angus & Robertson Publishers, Australia, 1982

Text published by arrangement with the copyright holders
Film Stills © Snowy River Production & Distribution Pty Ltd
Introduction © Angus & Robertson Publishers

National Library of Australia
Cataloguing-in-publication data.

Paterson, A. B. (Andrew Barton), 1864-1941.
  The man from Snowy River.

  ISBN 0 207 14794 9.

  I. Title.

A828'.209

Typeset in 12pt Announcement by Savage & Co. Pty Ltd
Printed in Hong Kong

FOREWORD

The poems and prose selections in this book, together with the magnificent photography, depict our grandfather's great love of the Snowy Mountains and surrounding countryside. His feeling for this area sprang from a boyhood spent at Illalong, near Yass. "The Man from Snowy River", perhaps his best known poem, is a tribute to the men and horses of the district, with which he was so well acquainted. He was, himself, a notable horseman and could appreciate the skill of the riders, in view of the difficulties of the terrain.

In his novel AN OUTBACK MARRIAGE, the station "Kuryong" is set in the Snowy region, and some descriptive passages from this work are included in the book.

It was to the Yass district that our grandfather returned in 1908, when he joined in the purchase of "Coodra Vale", Wee Jasper. He knew the risks attached to this way of life, as appears from his early poem "A Mountain Station" — "I bought a run . . . in country rough and ridgy . . .". Some years later, he returned to Sydney to resume his career in journalism.

In "Hillbillies", one of a series of reminiscences which he wrote in 1939 for the SYDNEY MORNING HERALD, he describes life at Coodra Vale — "40,000 acres, consisting mainly of country that had been left over after the rest of the world was made." Again, to use his own words, "The country was unfenced, and one could ride for miles and miles in the ranges seeing nothing but wild horses, wild cattle, wombats and wallaroos and hearing at night the chatter of the flying squirrels playing among the gum-tree blossoms." Wild horses were the inspiration for his poem "Brumby's Run".

His poems of the south are few, and are representative of his youth. Many of his other and later works are set in western New South Wales, his other great love.

The photographs illustrating this selection were taken while filming THE MAN FROM SNOWY RIVER. We believe our grandfather would have been as delighted with them as we are.

E.R.C. and P.G.H.

(NATIONAL LIBRARY OF AUSTRALIA)

INTRODUCTION

The Australian bush has become an enduring part of our social, economic and, especially, our literary traditions. Seventy years ago Dr C.E.W. Bean, noted historian and author, wrote:

*The Australian, one hundred or two hundred years hence, will
still live with the consciousness that, if he goes far enough back
over the hills and across the plains, he comes in the end to the
mysterious half desert country where men have to live the lives
of strong men. And the life of that mysterious country will
affect the Australian imagination much as the life of the sea
has affected that of the English.*

This creative philosophy has inspired much of the best of our prose and poetry and, for that matter, our films. And nobody in our literature has contributed more to these traditions than Andrew Barton Paterson, born in 1864 at Narambla, near Orange, the eldest of seven children of Andrew Paterson, a station owner and manager.

Young Barty Paterson had a typical bush boyhood which was best enjoyed from the age of five, after his father had moved to a station called Illalong in the Yass district of New South Wales.

He was, by his own admission, a lonely child, since he was twelve years older than his only brother. In a way this was the genesis of his lifelong love of the bush since, thereby, he turned for his pleasures and pastimes to the sights and sounds about him. The Yass district, apart from its scenic environment offered highly romantic possibilities for a young boy. The station at Illalong was on the main route between Sydney and Melbourne, along which came the exciting traffic of horsemen, bullock teams, drovers and especially coaches (the famous Cobb and Company coaching system was by 1870 at the peak of its popularity).

It was even more stirring to a young imagination that the gold-diggings of Lambing Flat (now called Young) were only a day's ride away and the gold escort came past twice a week with an armed trooper, rifle at the ready, riding in front and another in the box with the coachman. The word "bushranger" with its overtones of terror and fascination was always in the air.

And from these boyhood experiences, too, came the young Paterson's introduction to the great "characters" of the bush. There were the bullockies, with whom he made friends and who yarned with him and gave him demonstrations of their terrifying skill with their great whips. There were the drovers with their dusty herds and their myriad dogs. And there were the bush horsemen who loped by, ever ready to pass the time of day even with a small boy, and to enquire where tucker could be got. These were the bush types eventually to be projected into

The young Paterson — a city schoolboy.
After a couple of years at a colourful bush school at Binalong
where he sat with the nephews of bushrangers and the sons of navvies,
Paterson was sent to a Sydney prep school ("a nice quiet institution
where we were all little gentlemen") and later to Sydney Grammar School.

(COURTESY OF THE PATERSON FAMILY)

———

Paterson's ballads — the archetypes of Saltbush Bill, Clancy of the Overflow, the Man from Ironbark and Mulga Bill.

One New Year's Day the station rouseabout (a youth of eighteen) took the eight-year-old Paterson to the Bogolong picnic races nearby. (Bogolong, now Bookham, is on the Hume Highway between Sydney and Melbourne.) Bogolong, as Paterson recalled, was made up of two pubs with half-a-mile of road between. ". . . one pub," said the knowledgeable rouseabout, "to ketch the coves coming from Yass and the other to ketch the coves from Jugiong". The racecourse was some distance from the town, laid out through a gum and stringybark scrub; there was no grandstand; and the racehorses were tied to trees here and there. The men from Snowy River were there — wild, reckless riders; others, just as accomplished horsemen, from the rough Murrumbidgee country; Aboriginals, half-castes, sun-burned jackaroos, and a few townspeople from Yass and nearby centres.

The young Barty had ridden over on a pony with a light saddle; just before the main race, the Bogolong Town Plate, was run, he saw a tall Murrumbidgee horseman removing the saddle and putting it on his racehorse. The mountain man told him not to worry; the race was "ketch weights"; he therefore wanted to borrow the lightest saddle he could, and he promised the boy a ginger beer if his horse, Pardon, won. As Paterson later recalled:

> . . . Imagine then the excitement with which I watched
> Pardon's progress — watched him lying behind the leaders as
> they went out of sight behind the stringybark scrub; watched
> them come into sight again, with Pardon still lying third; and
> then the crowning moment as he drew away in the straight to
> win comfortably.

This episode was (as he admitted in later life) not only the origin of his famous poem, "Old Pardon, the Son of Reprieve"

> . . . And how he did come! It was splendid;
> He gained on them yards every bound,
> Stretching out like a greyhound extended,
> His girth laid right down on the ground . . .

but it was also his first experience of the daredevil horsemen of the Snowy and Murrumbidgee country. It also sowed the seeds of his lifelong passion for horses, horse riding and horse racing which was to see him become one of the most accomplished equestrians of his day (he won a steeplechase at Randwick as an amateur rider in 1895) and a nationally acclaimed polo player. And had he known it, it was to take him to the desert sands of Egypt in World War I.

Schooldays saw the young Paterson riding bareback four miles to the little bush school at Binalong. But at the age of eleven he was sent by his parents to Sydney Grammar School as a day boy — living with his grandmother Barton at Gladesville. Except for holiday periods he was not to return to the country to live until much later in life.

For after his six years at secondary school he went into a Sydney solicitor's office as an articled clerk. His grandmother, an educated and cultured woman, instilled into him a love of literature. Above all, by telling him endless stories of her pioneering days in the outback of the 1840s and 1850s, she kindled in him ideas of writing about the bush and its people.

Gradually Paterson changed from a shy and awkward bush boy into a young man whose wit, elegance of dress and manner and, especially, his prowess as a sportsman, made him a leader among the young Sydney men of his day. He was not only a first-class horseman, polo player and tennis player, but he became too a sailing and sculling enthusiast — for these were the days of the great Ned Trickett, Gipsy Beach and Harry Searle ("The Clarence Comet") who rowed, as world champions, on the Parramatta River.

Sydney in the 1880s was a thriving and exciting city and the suburbs were spreading out rapidly as a result of a boom in land development and building. But more than this, the young nation, though still a group of colonies, was developing its voice, its writers. Henry Kendall had sung of its beauties as he saw them, and Adam Lindsay Gordon, especially, had pointed the way to a form of literary bush ballad which united both country and city in a kind of self-conscious nationalism which looked particularly to horsemanship and bushcraft among the traditions of outback life. Paterson, barely out of his teens, decided that the time had come when he too could write verse of this kind.

A medium for the effective awakening of Australia to the fact that there was a national literature, although it was first a literature of the bush, was already in existence. In 1880 the BULLETIN had been founded under the vigorous editorship of J. F. Archibald who consistently and persistently looked for and encouraged Australian writers. It had flourished, and by the 1890s it enjoyed the widest readership of any journal in Australia. Under Archibald's influence, the BULLETIN first published the writings of Henry Lawson, Barcroft Boake, Louis Becke and others. Paterson submitted his first verses in 1885; though they were mediocre by his later standards they nevertheless attracted the personal attention of Archibald who encouraged the young poet to write about the subject he best knew — the bush and its people.

It was good advice. A cultural upheaval was taking place and the nation was thirsting for its own literature. Everything Australian suddenly became worth writing about: the outback, the diggings, the selections, the stock routes, the wheat fields, even the seaports and the slums. It was against this background that Paterson was launched as a bush balladist for it was in 1888 that the BULLETIN published his "Old Pardon, the Son of Reprieve" — the first of his ballads to attract significant attention. Paterson had adopted the pen-name "The Banjo", after what he described as a "so-called racehorse" his family had owned at Illalong.

By the early 1890s Paterson's ballads had become a popular feature of the BULLETIN. He was now a practising solicitor (which was probably why he had decided to use a pseudonym for his writing. "Now remember girls," his proud mother said to his equally proud sisters when they heard the news, "Barty's opinion is worth six-and-eightpence!"). Along with such celebrated and popular writers as Henry Lawson, Roderic Quinn, E. J. Brady, Edward Dyson and Victor Daley, Paterson's contributions were eagerly awaited and in this period he wrote "Clancy of the Overflow", "The Man from Snowy River" (which aroused enormous interest) and such humorous masterpieces as "The Geebung Polo Club" and "The Man from Ironbark".

*Paterson's love and knowledge of horses is recorded in his
verse but he was himself a successful horseman, polo player and huntsman.
Mounted on Namesake, he clears the last hurdle to win the Polo Hurdles, May 1897.*

(COURTESY OF THE PATERSON FAMILY)

————

Interestingly enough one of Paterson's fellow writers of the BULLETIN group was Harry "The Breaker" Morant. Although they met on a number of occasions and corresponded when Morant "went outback", Paterson had no high regard for Morant. Nevertheless after the latter's tragic death by court martial at the Boer War, Paterson wrote (one supposes, as charitably as he thought he could): ". . . I find it hard to believe that he killed anybody for gain. Reckless ne'er-do-well he was, but one finds it very difficult to think of him as a murderer."

It was not until 1895, when the famous Australian publishing firm of Angus & Robertson produced THE MAN FROM SNOWY RIVER AND OTHER VERSES (the first collected edition of his poems) that Paterson's identity was revealed. He became a celebrity overnight. It was a nine-day wonder in the colony that this tall, quiet and handsome young solicitor, already well known in Sydney's social and sporting circles, was "The Banjo". The book of verses sold in thousands in the next few weeks — and its popularity over all the years that have followed up to the present day has been a phenomenon of Australian book publishing.

At Jindabyne on a fishing trip.

(NATIONAL LIBRARY OF AUSTRALIA)

————

At the time of its publication, the success of THE MAN FROM SNOWY RIVER AND OTHER VERSES was directly related to the lack of other forms of communication competing with the printed word, and the formidable influence of the BULLETIN throughout most of settled Australia. When Paterson's identity was revealed, this success was undoubtedly assisted by his reputation as a prominent young Sydney man-about-town, sportsman and inter-colony polo player. Finally, it was helped by the fact that verse in his day (especially ballads of action) was as much spoken or sung as it was read, and thereby was an accepted means of entertainment in city and country. Since Paterson's ballads (and none more so than "The Man from Snowy River") were so obviously suited to recitation, his success was certain.

One of the direct influences of the popularity of Paterson's published verse, not only in 1895 but in ensuing years, was that it helped to establish the bushman in the national imagination as a romantic and traditional figure. At the turn of the century, as Russel Ward has written in THE AUSTRALIAN LEGEND, the bushman "had more influence on the manners and mores of the city-dweller than the latter had on his". He remains the nearest to the "noble frontiersman" that we shall ever have in our history. And the Man from Snowy River and Clancy of the Overflow became national symbols of the bushman/horserider now enshrined in our cultural mythology.

Soon after the publication of THE MAN FROM SNOWY RIVER AND OTHER VERSES, while on holidays near Winton in Queensland, Paterson wrote "Waltzing Matilda", the ballad for which he is best known not only in Australia but in many parts of the world. For the next few years he continued to write ballads, as well as many prose pieces and sketches for the BULLETIN wherein he demonstrated with many touches of quiet humour an acute observation of the people of the bush and their foibles. But he was becoming increasingly discontented with city life. He made several trips to north Queensland and the Northern Territory and wrote entertainingly of the opportunities offered by these parts for new experiences and adventure. And he began seriously to think of journalism rather than law as a future career.

The decision was largely made for him with the outbreak of the Boer War. In November 1899 he sailed for South Africa with the New South Wales Lancers as the officially accredited war correspondent for the SYDNEY MORNING HERALD and the Melbourne AGE. By January 1900 he was in the thick of all the actions in which the Lancers were involved against the Boers and he sent back throughout the year a series of exciting and vividly written despatches. He covered General French's relief of Kimberley, the surrender of General Cronje and the capture of Bloemfontein, the fighting round Johannesburg and the taking of Pretoria. These and other war experiences saw him develop into a first-class journalist. His brilliant work as a war reporter attracted the attention of Reuter's and he was appointed as a correspondent for this world-famous international news organization.

Yet, while he was gaining valuable experience as a newspaperman, Paterson remained a writer who found the best material for his verse and prose in personalities and men of action. So it was that he recorded in his Boer War experiences memorable pen pictures of the celebrities he met. These included Winston Churchill, Lord Roberts, French and other military leaders. Most of all he admired Haig and Allenby (then relatively junior officers) and he forecast greatness for them. But perhaps the most affectionate and, from the literary standpoint, the most useful relationship established by Paterson in South Africa was with Rudyard Kipling whom he met in March 1900 in Bloemfontein. He found they had much in common in their attitudes to writing, and of course in their love of the ballad idiom, and they became firm friends. Later, in his book of autobiographical sketches, HAPPY DISPATCHES, Paterson, always first and foremost an Australian, recorded his highest compliment to Kipling: ". . . You could have dumped Kipling down in a splitters' camp in the backblocks of Australia and he would have been quite at home; and would have gone away leaving the impression that he was a decent sort of bloke that asked a lot of questions."

Back in Australia at the end of 1900, Paterson, now firmly smitten with the wanderlust, yearned for more overseas experiences. In mid-1901 he was off again, this time to China and the Boxer Rebellion. He met and admired "Chinese" Morrison, the famous Australian adventurer, but the Boxer war had ended, so he set off to London where he renewed his friendship with Kipling and met again a former colleague of his BULLETIN days, Phil May, the noted cartoonist.

Again, back in Australia in 1902, he published his second book of verse, RIO GRANDE'S LAST RACE AND OTHER VERSES, and, at the age of thirty-nine, married a Tenterfield girl, Alice Walker. She was an accomplished horse-woman and a keen sportswoman and shared many of his interests. It was to be a happy and enduring marriage.

But now Paterson entered on the third phase of his career, this time as a successful newspaper editor. In January 1903 he was appointed editor of the EVENING NEWS, the more important of Sydney's two afternoon newspapers.

As an editor he is affectionately remembered for his sense of humour, his love of a good yarn, especially with visitors from the bush who were treated like long-lost brothers, and for his kindliness to his colleagues and employees. In 1905 he published his collection of early Australian ballads, OLD BUSH SONGS, which remains an authoritative source book even in the present day. In 1906 his first novel, AN OUTBACK MARRIAGE, appeared. The story was a conventional one, but descriptions of the bush and of some of its minor characters made the book readable.

By 1908, however, the call of the bush had become too strong. He sold up in the city, left his editor's desk and with his wife and two children took over a property called Coodra Vale in the rugged Wee Jasper district. Here he was on the fringe of his beloved Snowy River country and his few years here were happy ones. He sang of them in such ballads as "The Road to Hogan's Gap" and "The Mountain Squatter"

Here in my mountain home,
On rugged hills and steep
I sit and watch you come
O Riverina sheep . . .

Mr and Mrs A. B. Paterson, daughter Grace, and Peter Docherty
their Australian Terrier. A charming shot taken about 1904 at the
family home, Westhall, which still stands in Queen Street, Woollahra.

(COURTESY OF THE PATERSON FAMILY)

and perhaps with thoughts of ''The Man from Snowy River'', made particular reference to the expert horsemanship that the terrain demanded:

These Riverina cracks,
  They do not care to ride
The half-inch hanging tracks
  Along the mountain side.

Their horses shake with fear
  When loosened boulders go
With leaps like startled deer
  Down the gulfs below.

But this inaccessible and hostile terrain, and the snow, eventually got the better of him and retreating, as he said, like Napoleon from Moscow, he took over a wheat farm at Grenfell in 1911. But this did not suit his lifestyle and by 1912 he was back in Sydney earning a living as a freelance journalist.

At the outbreak of World War I Paterson, at the age of fifty, did his best to get into active service, but without success. He compromised by accepting a commission as an AIF Lieutenant in the first Australian Remount Unit. This was a job after Paterson's heart. The squadrons, one of which he commanded, were made up of rough riders — jackaroos, horse-breakers from the outback, ex-jockeys, and buck-jumping riders from country shows. Paterson wrote of them as ''the best lot of men that were ever got together to deal with rough horses''.

By the beginning of 1916 Paterson, now promoted to the rank of Captain, had arrived in Egypt. His work included the control of horses bought by the Army buyers all over the world. In whatever state they were in he had to break them in or subdue them and eventually bring them to the stage of training and docility where they could be mounted at will by a heavily armed trooper. By the end of 1916 he had reached the rank of Major and his enthusiasm for and efficiency with horses earned him the respect and affection of fighting men throughout the Middle East. In later years he calculated that 50,000 horses and 10,000 mules had passed through his hands.

On his return to Australia at the end of the war Paterson and his family set up house in the eastern suburbs of Sydney where they remained for the rest of their lives. Paterson was immediately in touch with his publishers, Angus & Robertson, for while he was in Egypt they had published a number of his short stories and sketches under the title of THREE ELEPHANT POWER AND OTHER STORIES and also his third volume of ballads, SALTBUSH BILL, J.P. AND OTHER VERSE. He was now keen that the first collected edition of his verse

Coodra Station. In 1908, to satisfy a continual hankering to go back to the land, Paterson sold his Woollahra home and bought the 40,000 acre Coodra Station in his beloved Upper Murrumbidgee country.

(COURTESY OF THE PATERSON FAMILY)

———————

should be issued and he worked closely with his publishers on its contents, which included most of what had appeared in his earlier volumes. It was published in 1921. At the same time he had been interesting himself in journalism again and he did freelance work for various Sydney newspapers until, in 1921, he was offered and accepted the editorship of the SPORTSMAN. This was a weekly journal devoted largely to horse racing, but it included a coverage of most other sports.

There is no doubt that the years in which he edited the SPORTSMAN were among Paterson's happiest. He loved thoroughbred racing and sporting journalism, and, in addition to his editing duties, he reported the Sydney races each week for the newspaper TRUTH.

In 1930, at the age of sixty-six, Paterson left the SPORTSMAN to concentrate on freelance writing again. He also did a good deal of broadcasting for the ABC about his life and adventures. He produced in 1933 a charming collection of rhymes for children entitled THE ANIMALS NOAH FORGOT, which was illustrated by his friend and admirer Norman Lindsay, and a year later his autobiographical reminiscences HAPPY DISPATCHES appeared.

He lectured, wrote and lived the life of a respected Sydney clubman and man-about-town during the 1930s. In January 1939 he was awarded the CBE for his services to Australian literature (along with similar honours to Professor Walter Murdoch and Mrs Aeneas Gunn). "The Commonwealth does well," wrote the SYDNEY MORNING HERALD in its leading article on the day, "to recommend royal recognition of the writers who interpret the life and spirit of this land."

Two years later Paterson died suddenly, after a short illness, on 14 February 1941, three days short of his seventy-seventh birthday.

Paterson was a much better prose writer than he has been given credit for. His animal pieces, some of which are collected in THREE ELEPHANT POWER AND OTHER STORIES, are often superbly entertaining and indeed many of his bush sketches invite comparison with some of Henry Lawson's stories. Paterson had an instinctive understanding of the foibles and philosophies of bush characters and he handled outback dialogue unerringly, as for instance in this passage from his novel, AN OUTBACK MARRIAGE:

Just as the coach was about to start a drover came out of the bar of the hotel, wiping his lips with the back of his hand. He stared vacantly about him, first up street and then down, looked hard at a post in front of the hotel and then stared up and down the street again. At last he walked over, and addressing the passengers in a body, said, "Did any of yous see e'er a horse anywheres? I left me prad here, an' he's gorn."

A bystander, languidly cutting up a pipeful of tobacco, jerked his elbow down the road.

"That old bloke took 'im," he said. "Old bloke that come in the coach. While yous was all talking in the pub he sneaks out here and nabs that 'orse, and away like a rabbit. See that dust on the plain? That's 'im!"

The drover looked helplessly out over the stretch of plain. He seemed quite incapable of grappling with the problem.

"Took me horse, did he? Well I'm blowed! By Cripes!"

He had another good stare over the plain, and back at the party.

"My oath!" he added.

Then the natural stoicism of the bushman came to his aid and he said, in a resigned tone,

"Oh, well, anyways, I s'pose — s'pose he must have been in a hurry to go somewheres. I s'pose he'll fetch him back some time or other."

But Paterson's enduring greatness in Australian literature stems from his ballads. He is our best known and most revered folk singer, and he had the instinct of the folk singer to shape the material he had gathered over the length and breadth of Australia into its most telling fashion and give it a national vogue. In simple words he made a balladry of the scattered lives of back-country Australians who thought nobody noticed them and until then had scarcely noticed themselves.

It was a varied, interesting and above all, lovable country that Paterson revealed to the people of his and later generations. A country of drought, dust and heat — yes, but a country which had her own beauty and moments of gentleness. Paterson found the bush's own music in the western plains — that great hinterland between the upper reaches of the Lachlan River to the north and the Eumerella to the south — but then he was equally the poet of the outback from the Northern Territory and the Queensland downs to the Snowy country of the south. To him it was all "the land of lots o' time" — a country of unending variety and changes, and yet so vast a country indeed that the lonely rider was seen as "a speck upon the waste of plain".

In these settings then, Paterson opened his heart to the land and its people; the teamsters of his youth

> . . . out on the Castlereagh, when they meet
> with a week of rain,
> And the wagon sinks to its axle-tree, deep down
> on the black-soil plain,
> When the bullocks wade in a sea of mud, and strain
> at the load of wool
> And the cattle-dogs at the bullocks' heels
> are biting to make them pull . . .

and the itinerant bushman in search of work

> I'm travelling down the Castlereagh, and I'm
> a station-hand,
> I'm handy with the ropin' pole, I'm handy
> with the brand,
> And I can ride a rowdy colt, or swing
> the axe all day,
> But there's no demand for a station-hand
> along the Castlereagh.

Major A.B. Paterson of the Remount service, Moascar, Egypt.
The American war correspondent Kermit Roosevelt met Paterson at this time and
described him as "... a man who has lived everything that he has written. At different periods
of his life he has dived for pearls in the islands, herded sheep, broken broncos and known every
chance and change in Australian station life ... A recent feat about which I heard much mention
was when he drove 300 mules straight through Cairo without losing a single animal, conclusively
proving his argument against those who had contested that such a thing could not be done ..."

(COURTESY OF THE PATERSON FAMILY)

———

In many ways Paterson was as much a poet as balladist and the two need not be separated. H. M. Green, doyen of Australian literary historians, observed that "the quality that in the end he stands by is after all a poetic quality". And one of our foremost ballad authorities, John Manifold, always maintained that Paterson was "a far richer and more subtle poet" than he has been given credit for. Certainly in lines like these:

> *Like mariners calling the roll of their number*
> *The sea-fowl put out to the infinite deep.*
> *And far overhead — singing softly to slumber —*
> *Worn out by their watching the stars fall asleep.*

or in his magnificent invocation to the black swans:

O ye wild black swans, 'twere a world of wonder
　　For awhile to join in your westward flight,
With the stars above and the dim earth under,
　　Through the cooling air of the glorious night.
As we swept along on our pinions winging,
　　We should catch the chime of a church-bell ringing,
Or the distant note of a torrent singing,
　　Or the far-off flash of a station light.

he caught some of the essential poetry of our coastline and hinterland. But though that is an aspect of Paterson's writing that should not be forgotten, one accepts that, in the popular imagination, he was and remains best known for his lines that tell of action and adventure. A.J. Quiller Couch wrote in his Introduction to THE OXFORD BOOK OF BALLADS that the way to define a ballad is to quote lines that have the ring of balladry. And it is in Paterson's ballads of horses and horsemen that this is most true — where the landscape of action and the action itself combine most tellingly. And nowhere is this truer than of his "The Man from Snowy River". Paterson, a magnificent horseman himself, left little doubt that for him the action of the saddle was the finest possible evocation of the adventure and challenge of the outback — of the plains and, especially, of the mountains:

Then fast the horseman followed, where the gorges
　　　deep and black
　　Resounded to the thunder of their tread,
And the stockwhips woke the echoes and they fiercely
　　　answered back
　　From cliffs and crags that beetled overhead,
And upward, ever upward, the wild horses
　　　held their way,
　　Where mountain ash and kurrajong grew wide . . .

"The Man from Snowy River" is probably the most famous literary ballad in our literature. Among other things it set the seal on Paterson's achievements as a myth-maker, in this case going far beyond his own expectations. The celebrated ride, much more than being talked about only by the bush folk

> . . . down by Kosciusko where the pine-clad ridges raise
> Their torn and rugged battlements on high,
> Where the air is clear as crystal,
>   and the white stars fairly blaze
> At midnight in the cold and frosty sky,
> And where around the Overflow the reedbeds
>   sweep and sway
> To the breezes, and the rolling plains are wide . . .

has become a legend not only throughout Australia but in a good many other parts of the world as well.

All this arose from Paterson's remarkable ability to create the larger-than-life; as he had long observed, the stock-in-trade of the tellers of yarns round the camp-fires, in bush pubs, on lonely droving trails. Mulga Bill's epic bicycle ride and the Man from Ironbark's ordeal in the city barber's chair were the humorous manifestations of Paterson's gift, but the Man from Snowy River is his most dramatic and best-remembered creation.

It is said that Paterson with a companion, sometime in 1890, on a visit to the Snowy Mountains area, camped at the hut of one Jack Riley at his lonely outpost on a cattle station bordering Mount Kosciusko. Riley, whose reputation as a fearless rider and stockman was almost legendary in the district, is said to have told Paterson a story of a colt that "got away" in the mountains. In 1892 the ballad appeared; not unnaturally Riley's claims to be the original Man from Snowy River have been consistently argued. When he died in 1914 a headstone was erected on his grave in Corryong (Victoria) giving him the title.

But the claims of other famous riders for the honour have also been argued. There was Lachie Cochrane, a well-known bushman of the Snowy area who died in Cootamundra in 1922. Another aspirant was Owen Cummins who, as a young man, established a formidable reputation as a rider on the Bogong High Plains before going to the Northern Territory to become a boundary rider on the Wave Hill cattle station. Other claimants for the title include "Hell-fire" Jack Clarke, noted bushman and rider of the Adaminaby country; McEacharn of the Thredbo; George Hedger of Numbla Vale; and Jim Spencer of Jindabyne (who, it is said, was personally known to Paterson).

But all of this, as it transpires, was the result of Paterson, the myth-maker, at work. As he wrote a few years before his death:

Aged about 75, Paterson around the time he was awarded the CBE.

(COURTESY OF THE PATERSON FAMILY)

"The Man from Snowy River" was written to describe the cleaning up of the wild horses in my own district. To make a job of it I had to create a character, to imagine a man who could ride better than anybody else, and where could he come from except from the Snowy? And what sort of horse would he ride except a half-thoroughbred mountain pony?

I felt sure there must have been a Man from Snowy River and I was right. They have turned up from all the mountain districts — men who did exactly the same ride and could give you chapter and verse for every mile they descended and every creek they crossed. It was no small satisfaction that there really had been a Man from Snowy River — more than one of them . . .

The poem has been set to music and in more recent years has been transcribed on to gramophone record by some of our best known actors and verse-speakers. But over sixty years ago the title of "The Man from Snowy River" caught the imagination of a pioneer Australian film-maker of those days, Beaumont Smith. A showman and theatrical entrepreneur of World War I years, he began making films in 1917, producing a series of low-budget films shot in bush backgrounds in various parts of Australia, about the Hayseed family — a precursor of the Dad and Dave films of a later generation.

Beaumont Smith was seized with the romantic possibilities of "The Man from Snowy River" and in 1919 he set out for Los Angeles, hoping to recruit a cast of expatriate Australian actors in Hollywood and to make a film with an "Australian" background provided by the gumtrees growing in California.

Having found this impracticable he returned to Australia and shot the film on location at Mulgoa to the south-west of Sydney. In the cast was that stalwart of early Australian films, Tal Ordell. For his heroine Beaumont Smith "discovered" a girl in a Sydney millinery shop and gave her the screen pseudonym of Stella Southern.

Apart from Paterson's title, the film bore no resemblance to the poem. It was a conventional story of an outback romance; of the rivalry between two station owners, culminating in a horse race to decide the issue, with the required happy ending. Paterson in his writings never made any reference to the film. Nevertheless it seemed to have been a commercial success. A journal of the day described it as "the best Australian film yet made", and advertising hoardings outside a Brisbane cinema described it as having "a kick like a kangaroo" and being "as sunny as Queensland . . . as big as Australia".

Now the wheel has turned full circle and once again "The Man from Snowy River" takes its place in this late twentieth century renaissance of the Australian film industry. One can be sure that all lovers of Paterson's ballads will wish every success to the film and the film-makers who went on location to the very areas that Paterson loved so dearly. And one can believe that the spirit of Paterson would applaud the imagination of those who have sought to re-create this epic of horsemanship.

Come to think of it, Paterson as a young man, handsome, an accomplished horseman and athlete, would have been ideally cast as the hero of the film. For one recalls the late Norman Lindsay's pen portrait of Paterson in his early thirties and at the height of his prowess:

> . . . It is rare that a superior spirit is given a superior casing,
> but Paterson had it. A tall man with a finely built, muscular
> body, moving with the ease of perfectly co-ordinated reflexes.
> Black hair, dark eyes, a long, finely articulated nose, an ironic
> mouth, a dark pigmentation of skin . . . His eyes, as eyes must
> be, were his most distinctive feature, slightly hooded, with a
> glance that looked beyond one as he talked . . .

It is appropriate that the film, THE MAN FROM SNOWY RIVER, should be a further tribute to a great Australian who helped create the Australian legend and yet, in his lifetime, was a living part of that legend.

— Clement Semmler

BRUMBY'S RUN

BRUMBY'S RUN

It lies beyond the Western Pines
  Beneath the sinking sun,
And not a survey mark defines
  The bounds of "Brumby's Run".

On odds and ends of mountain land,
  On tracks of range and rock
Where no one else can make a stand
  Old Brumby rears his stock.

A wild, unhandled lot they are
    Of every shape and breed.
They venture out 'neath moon and star
    Along the flats to feed;

But, when the dawn makes pink the sky
    And steals along the plain,
The Brumby horses turn and fly
    Back to the hills again.

The traveller by the mountain-track
   May hear their hoof-beats pass,
And catch a glimpse of brown and black
   Dim shadows on the grass.

The eager stock-horse pricks his ears,
   And lifts his head on high
In wild excitement, when he hears
   The Brumby mob go by.

Old Brumby asks no price or fee
    O'er all his wide domains:
The man who yards his stock is free
    To keep them for his pains.

So, off to scour the mountain side
    With eager eyes aglow,
To strongholds where the wild mobs hide
    The gully-rakers go.

A rush of horses through the trees,
    A red shirt making play;
A sound of stockwhips on the breeze,
    They vanish far away!

· · · · ·

Ah, me! before our day is done
We long with bitter pain
To ride once more on Brumby's Run
And yard his mob again.

THE OLD STATION

THE OLD STATION
from *AN OUTBACK MARRIAGE,* 1906

The homestead itself had originally consisted of the two-roomed slab hut, which had been added to from time to time. Kitchen, outhouses, bachelors' quarters, saddle-rooms, and store-rooms had been built on in a kind of straggling quadrangle, with many corners and unexpected doorways and passages . . . . The original building was still the principal living-room . . .and a wide veranda ran all along the front.

Here and there clumps of willows and stately poplars waved in the breeze. In the clear, dry air all colours were startlingly vivid, and round the nearer foothills wonderful lights and shadows played and shifted, while sometimes a white fleece of mist would drift slowly across a distant hill, like a film of snowy lace on the face of a beautiful woman. Away behind the foothills were the grand old mountains, with their snow-clad tops gleaming in the sun.

In some parts of Australia it is difficult to tell summer from winter; but up in this mountain country each season had its own attractions. In the spring the flats were green with lush grass, speckled with buttercups and bachelors' buttons, and the willows put out their new leaves, and all manner of shy dry-scented bush flowers bloomed on the ranges; and the air was full of the song of birds and the calling of animals. Then came summer, when never a cloud decked the arch of blue sky, and all animated nature drew into the shade of big trees until the evening breeze sprang up, bringing sweet scents of the dry grass and ripening grain. In autumn, the leaves of the English trees turned all tints of yellow and crimson, and the grass in the paddocks went brown; and the big bullock teams worked from dawn till dark, hauling in their loads of hay from the cultivation paddocks.

But most beautiful of all was winter, when logs blazed in the huge fireplaces, and frosts made the ground crisp, and the stock, long-haired and shaggy, came snuffling round the stables, picking up odds and ends of straw; when the grey, snow-clad mountains looked but a stone's throw away in the intensely clear air, and the wind brought a colour to the cheeks and a tingling to the blood that made life worth living.

THE MAN FROM SNOWY RIVER

THE MAN FROM SNOWY RIVER

There was movement at the station, for the word had passed around
　　That the colt from old Regret had got away,
And had joined the wild bush horses — he was worth a thousand
　　　　pound,
　　So all the cracks had gathered to the fray.
All the tried and noted riders from the stations near and far
　　Had mustered at the homestead overnight,
For the bushmen love hard riding where the wild bush horses are,
　　And the stock-horse snuffs the battle with delight.

There was Harrison, who made his pile when Pardon won the cup,
    The old man with his hair as white as snow;
But few could ride beside him when his blood was fairly up —
    He would go wherever horse and man could go.
And Clancy of the Overflow came down to lend a hand,
    No better horseman ever held the reins;
For never horse could throw him while the saddle-girths would stand —
    He learnt to ride while droving on the plains.

And one was there, a stripling on a small and weedy beast;
　　He was something like a racehorse undersized,
With a touch of Timor pony — three parts thoroughbred at least —
　　And such as are by mountain horsemen prized.
He was hard and tough and wiry — just the sort that won't say die —
　　There was courage in his quick impatient tread;
And he bore the badge of gameness in his bright and fiery eye,
　　And the proud and lofty carriage of his head.

But still so slight and weedy, one would doubt his power to stay,
    And the old man said, "That horse will never do
For a long and tiring gallop — lad, you'd better stop away,
    Those hills are far too rough for such as you."
So he waited, sad and wistful — only Clancy stood his friend —
    "I think we ought to let him come," he said;
"I warrant he'll be with us when he's wanted at the end,
    For both his horse and he are mountain bred.

"He hails from Snowy River, up by Kosciusko's side,
Where the hills are twice as steep and twice as rough;
Where a horse's hoofs strike firelight from the flint stones every stride,
The man that holds his own is good enough.

And the Snowy River riders on the mountains make their home,
    Where the river runs those giant hills between;
I have seen full many horsemen since I first commenced to roam,
    But nowhere yet such horsemen have I seen."

So he went; they found the horses by the big mimosa clump,
  They raced away towards the mountain's brow,
And the old man gave his orders, "Boys, go at them from the jump,
  No use to try for fancy riding now.
And, Clancy, you must wheel them, try and wheel them to the right.
  Ride boldly, lad, and never fear the spills,
For never yet was rider that could keep the mob in sight,
  If once they gain the shelter of those hills."

So Clancy rode to wheel them — he was racing on the wing
    Where the best and boldest riders take their place,
And he raced his stock-horse past them, and he made the ranges ring
    With the stockwhip, as he met them face to face.
Then they halted for a moment, while he swung the dreaded lash,
    But they saw their well-loved mountain full in view,
And they charged beneath the stockwhip with a sharp and sudden
        dash,
    And off into the mountain scrub they flew.

Then fast the horsemen followed, where the gorges deep and black
  Resounded to the thunder of their tread,
And the stockwhips woke the echoes, and they fiercely answered back
  From cliffs and crags that beetled overhead.

And upward, ever upward, the wild horses held their way,
    Where mountain ash and kurrajong grew wide;
And the old man muttered fiercely, "We may bid the mob good day,
    No man can hold them down the other side."

When they reached the mountain's summit, even Clancy took a pull —
   It well might make the boldest hold their breath;
The wild hop scrub grew thickly, and the hidden ground was full
   Of wombat holes, and any slip was death.

But the man from Snowy River let the pony have his head,
 And he swung his stockwhip round and gave a cheer,
And he raced him down the mountain like a torrent down its bed,
 While the others stood and watched in very fear.

He sent the flint-stones flying, but the pony kept his feet,
    He cleared the fallen timber in his stride,
And the man from Snowy River never shifted in his seat —
    It was grand to see that mountain horseman ride.
Through the stringy barks and saplings, on the rough and broken
        ground,
    Down the hillside at a racing pace he went;
And he never drew the bridle till he landed safe and sound
    At the bottom of that terrible descent.

He was right among the horses as they climbed the farther hill,
    And the watchers on the mountain, standing mute,
Saw him ply the stockwhip fiercely; he was right among them still,
    As he raced across the clearing in pursuit.

Then they lost him for a moment, where two mountain gullies met
     In the ranges — but a final glimpse reveals
On a dim and distant hillside the wild horses racing yet,
     With the man from Snowy River at their heels.

And he ran them single-handed till their sides were white with foam;
    He followed like a bloodhound on their track,
Till they halted, cowed and beaten; then he turned their heads for
        home,
    And alone and unassisted brought them back.
But his hardy mountain pony he could scarcely raise a trot,
    He was blood from hip to shoulder from the spur;
But his pluck was still undaunted, and his courage fiery hot,
    For never yet was mountain horse a cur.

And down by Kosciusko, where the pine-clad ridges raise
  Their torn and rugged battlements on high,
Where the air is clear as crystal, and the white stars fairly blaze
  At midnight in the cold and frosty sky,
And where around the Overflow the reed-beds sweep and sway
  To the breezes, and the rolling plains are wide,
The Man from Snowy River is a household word today,
  And the stockmen tell the story of his ride.

KING ALFRED'S COLLEGE
LIBRARY

Mounted on Snowy River and leading The Shifter and Brunette (partly obscured). Paterson was proud of all three horses and recorded their triumphs in his photo album. Snowy River was twice awarded the Champion Polo Pony sash at Sydney Show and won two cigar races. The Shifter and Brunette came first and second respectively in the first Polo Cup to be run in New South Wales.
(COURTESY OF THE PATERSON FAMILY)